Football in America

YOUTH FOOTBALL

Robert Cooper

DiscoverRoo
An Imprint of Pop!
popbooksonline.com

abdobooks.com

Published by Pop!, a division of ABDO, PO Box 398166, Minneapolis, Minnesota 55439.

Printed in the United States of America, North Mankato, Minnesota.

052019
092019

THIS BOOK CONTAINS RECYCLED MATERIALS

Cover Photo: Shutterstock Images
Interior Photos: Shutterstock Images, 1, 5, 6–7, 8, 9, 14–15, 15, 20, 22, 23, 25, 28, 30; iStockphoto, 11, 12, 16 (player), 16–17 (background), 31; Charles Krupa/AP Images, 13; Tom E. Puskar/NFL Network/AP Images, 19; AP Images, 21; Paul Spinelli/AP Images, 26; Tom DiPace/AP Images, 27; Red Line Editorial, 29

Editor: Nick Rebman
Series Designer: Jake Nordby

Library of Congress Control Number: 2018964852

Publisher's Cataloging-in-Publication Data

Names: Cooper, Robert, author.

Title: Youth football / by Robert Cooper.

Description: Minneapolis, Minnesota : Pop!, 2020 | Series: Football in America | Includes online resources and index.

Identifiers: ISBN 9781532163807 (lib. bdg.) | ISBN 9781644940532 (pbk.) | ISBN 9781532165245 (ebook)

Subjects: LCSH: Football--Juvenile literature. | American football--Juvenile literature. | Youth league football--Juvenile literature. | Sports for children--Juvenile literature.

Classification: DDC 796.33262--dc23

TABLE OF CONTENTS

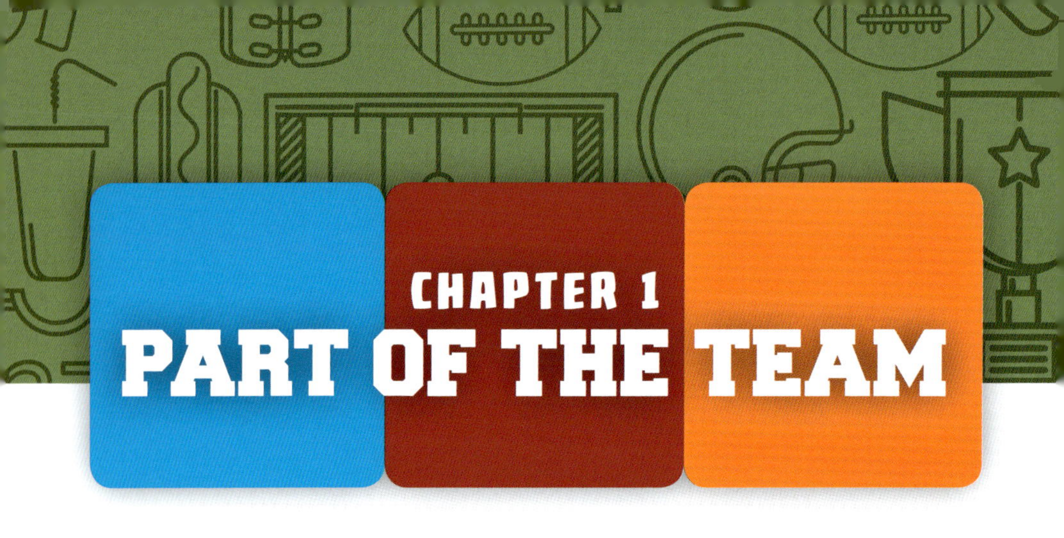

CHAPTER 1 PART OF THE TEAM

The running back swerves to the left. Next, he bolts to the right. Then he **sprints** down the field. It's a touchdown! The player will never forget this moment. Youth football is all about

A youth football player carries the ball down the field.

spending time with friends and enjoying the sport.

Football is one of the most popular youth sports in the United States. Kids don't have to know much about football before they start playing. They learn

A quarterback tosses the ball to a receiver.

about the sport while being part of the team. Everyone gets to play. It doesn't matter what the player's **ability** is.

The coach helps players work together to achieve a common goal.

Kids can learn many life lessons from playing football. For example, football teaches teamwork. To win a game, everyone on the team has to help out. The quarterback has to make

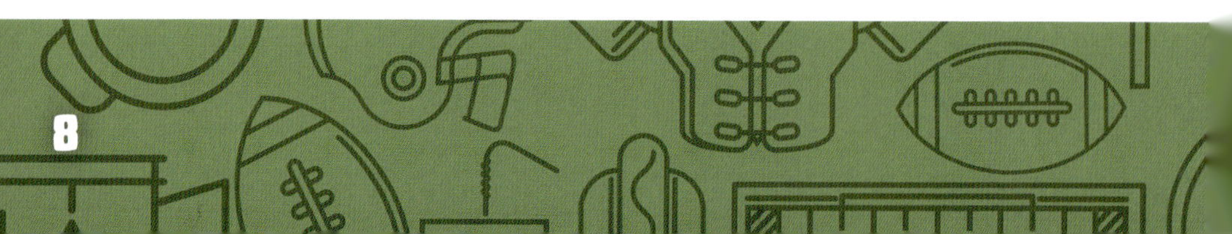

Teammates often build strong friendships.

good passes. The wide receiver has to catch. The defenders have to stop the other team.

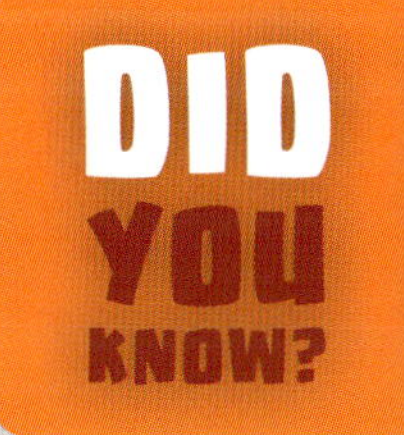

In 2015, more than one million kids played youth football.

CHAPTER 2
STARTING OUT

Kids start playing football as early as six years old. Many begin with flag football. It is a safer way to learn the rules of the game. In flag football, there is no tackling.

LEARN MORE HERE!

In flag football, defenders grab flags on the ball carrier's belt rather than tackling.

During practice, players may run between cones to work on their quickness.

Kids start by learning the game's **fundamentals**. The players need these skills to be successful on the field. They practice throwing and catching. They also work on running. They become faster and stronger.

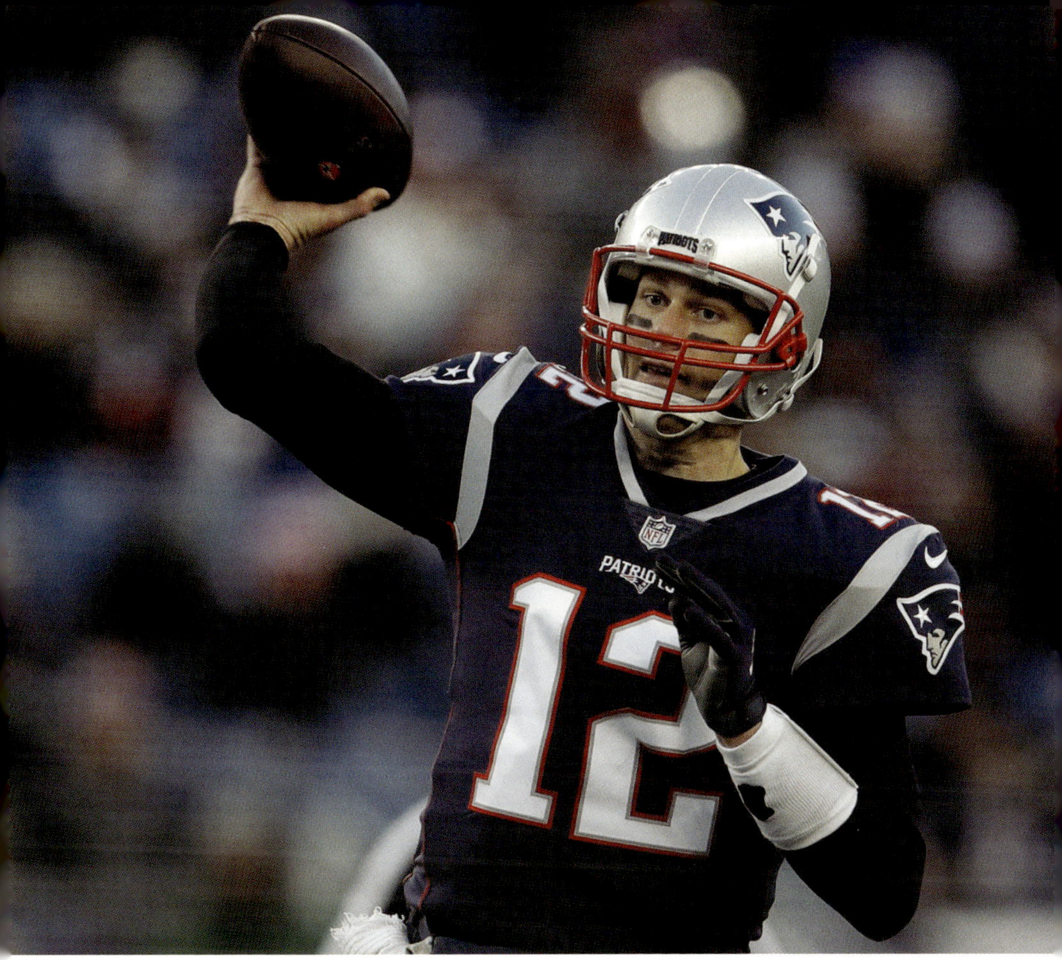

Tom Brady won his sixth Super Bowl after the 2018 season.

DID YOU KNOW?

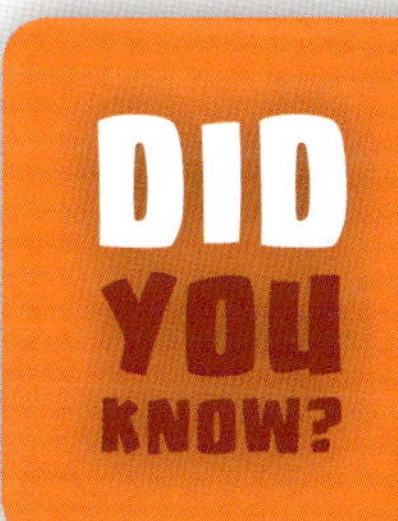

New England Patriots quarterback Tom Brady didn't start playing football until he was in high school.

During the **season**, players get to try all of the different positions. They throw passes as a quarterback.

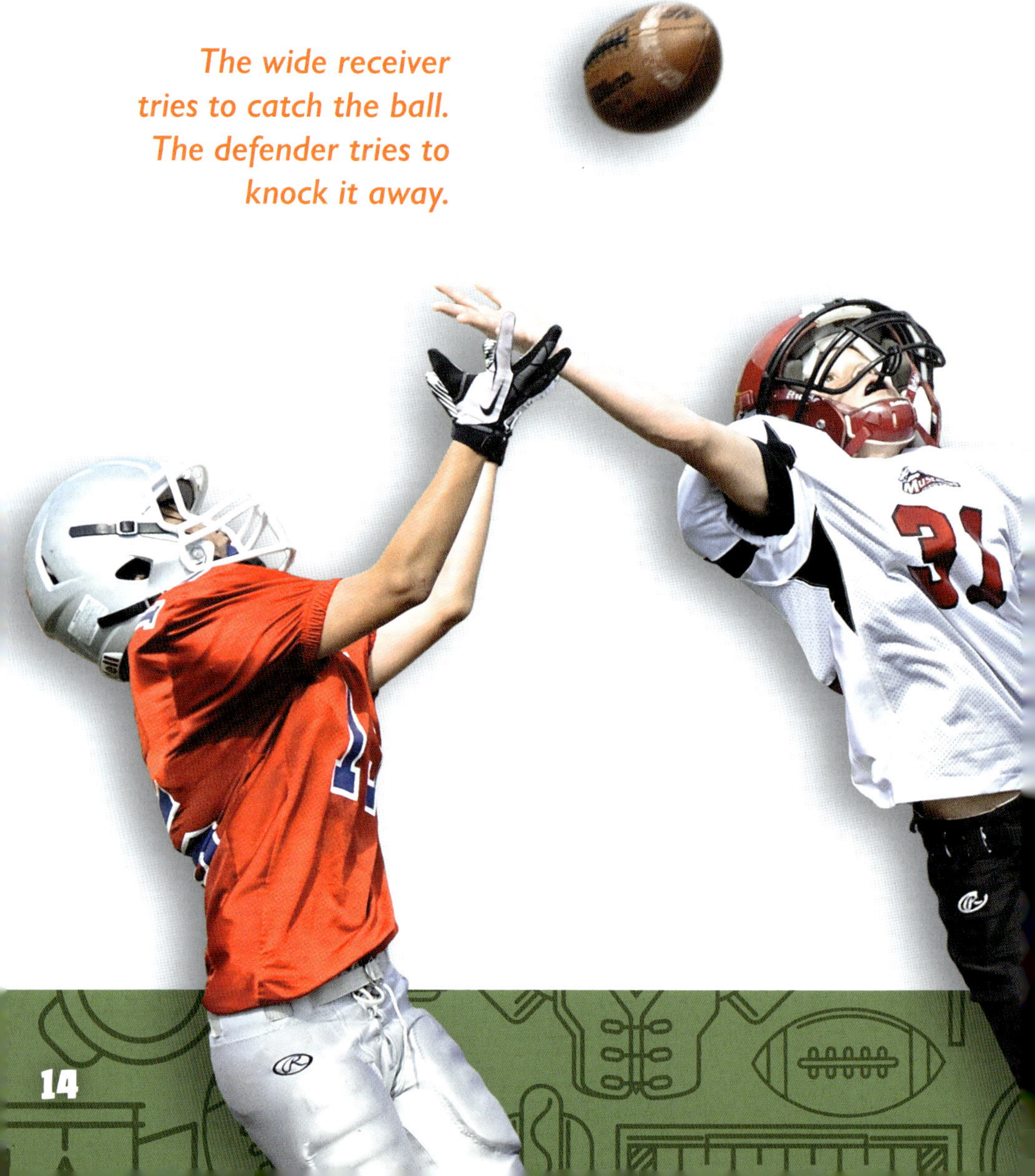

The wide receiver tries to catch the ball. The defender tries to knock it away.

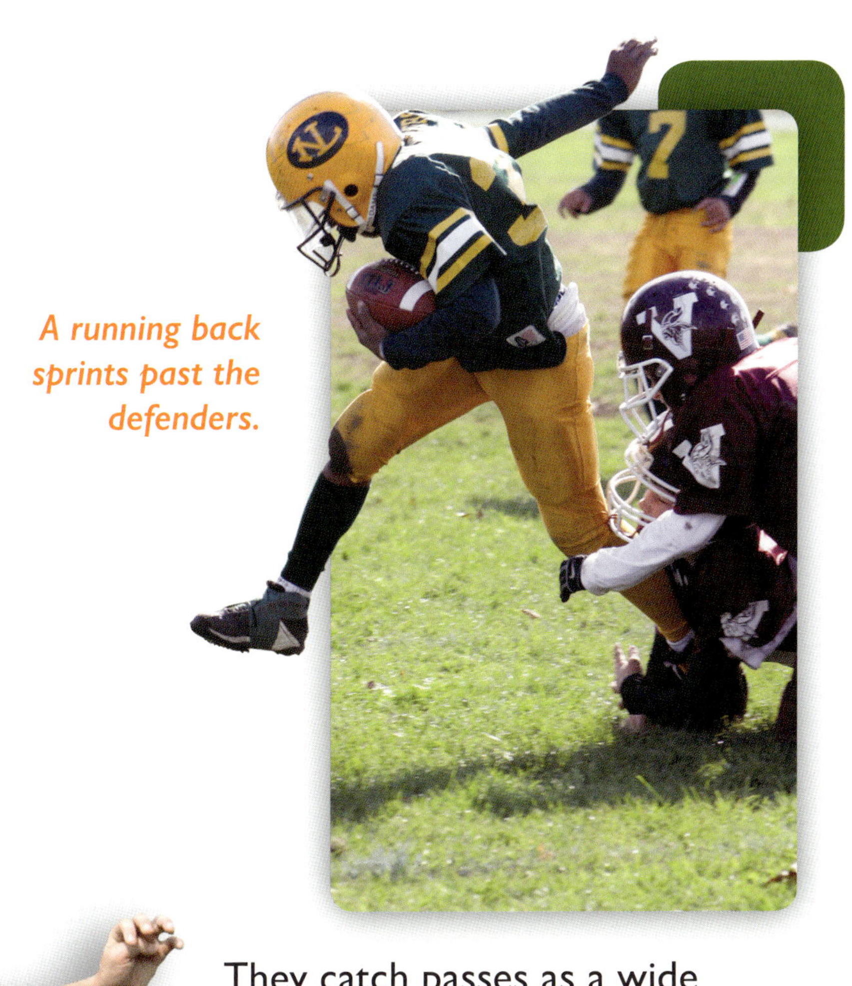

A running back sprints past the defenders.

They catch passes as a wide receiver. They also work on playing defense. Everyone gets a chance to play and enjoy the sport.

FLAG FOOTBALL POSITIONS

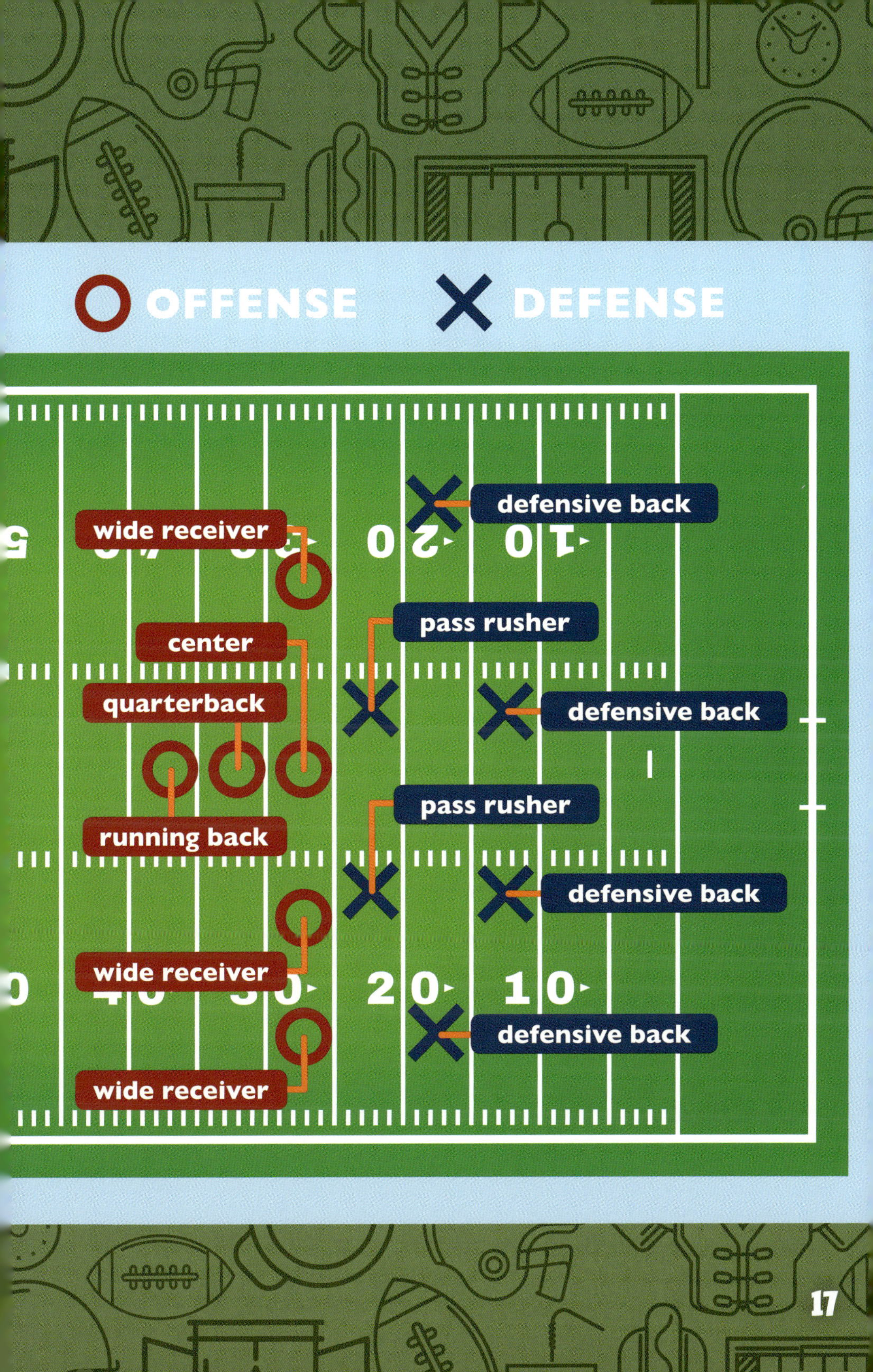
OFFENSE
DEFENSE
defensive back
wide receiver
pass rusher
center
quarterback
defensive back
pass rusher
running back
defensive back
wide receiver
defensive back
wide receiver
20
10
20
10

CHAPTER 3 STILL DEVELOPING

Tackle football can be dangerous. It often involves hard hits. Many doctors say kids should not start playing tackle football until the age of 12. That's because kids' bodies are still **developing**.

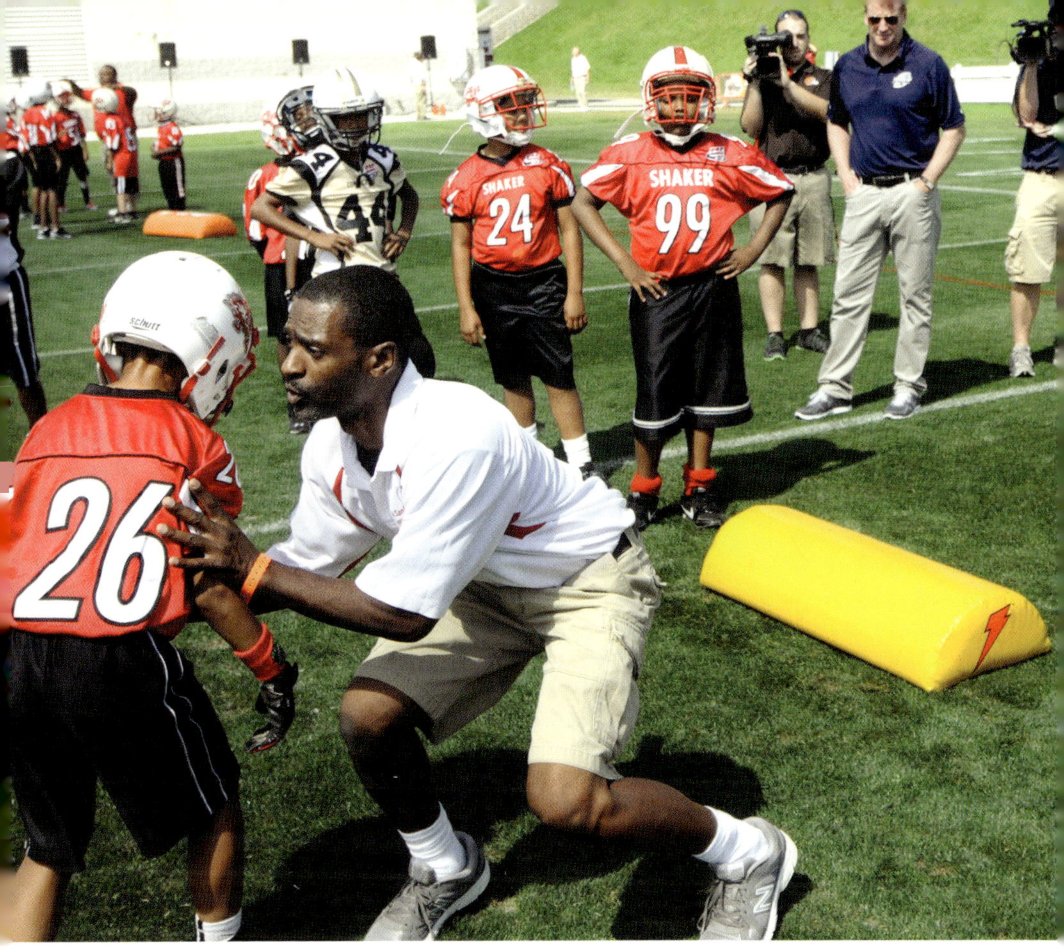

Players take part in a summer camp to improve their skills.

DID YOU KNOW?

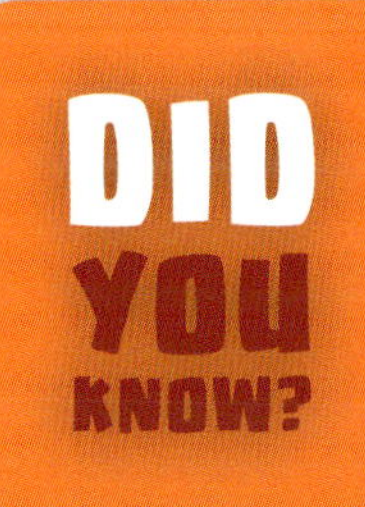

More than 100 NFL players held summer camps in 2018. These camps helped kids work on their football skills.

Coaches use pads to show players good tackling techniques.

Proper **technique** helps players avoid **injuries**. Coaches teach players how to tackle. Players learn how to stay low. They learn not to use their

heads when tackling. Players also learn the safest way to block.

Glenn Warner, also known as "Pop" Warner, was a college coach in the late 1800s and early 1900s.

POP WARNER

The most popular youth football league is called Pop Warner. Kids can play in Pop Warner starting when they are five years old. The league stops when players turn 16. The league has been going since 1929.

A wide receiver runs with the ball after making a catch.

Players start to focus on one or two positions as they get older. Many players focus on one offensive position and one defensive position. They work with coaches on specific skills for their position. For example, quarterbacks practice throwing. Defensive linemen work on tackling.

CHAPTER 4

BETTER WITH TIME

As players get older, football becomes more **competitive**. Kids begin playing on teams through their school. Coaches choose the top players for these teams.

COMPLETE AN ACTIVITY HERE!

Players who don't make the top team can still play on a lower-level team.

Focusing on one sport gives players more time to develop skills that are specific to football.

Many kids play several sports when they are young. But by middle school, some players decide to focus on football. They may play in 7-on-7 leagues when they're not playing tackle football. They also lift weights to stay in good shape.

Russell Wilson led the Seattle Seahawks to a Super Bowl victory in February 2014.

DID YOU KNOW?

Seattle Seahawks quarterback Russell Wilson played two sports all the way through college. He played baseball and football.

For most players, youth football goes through eighth grade. After that, players start high school football. The games become more competitive. But until then, kids can focus on learning about the game.

NUMBER OF KIDS PLAYING FOOTBALL IN THE UNITED STATES

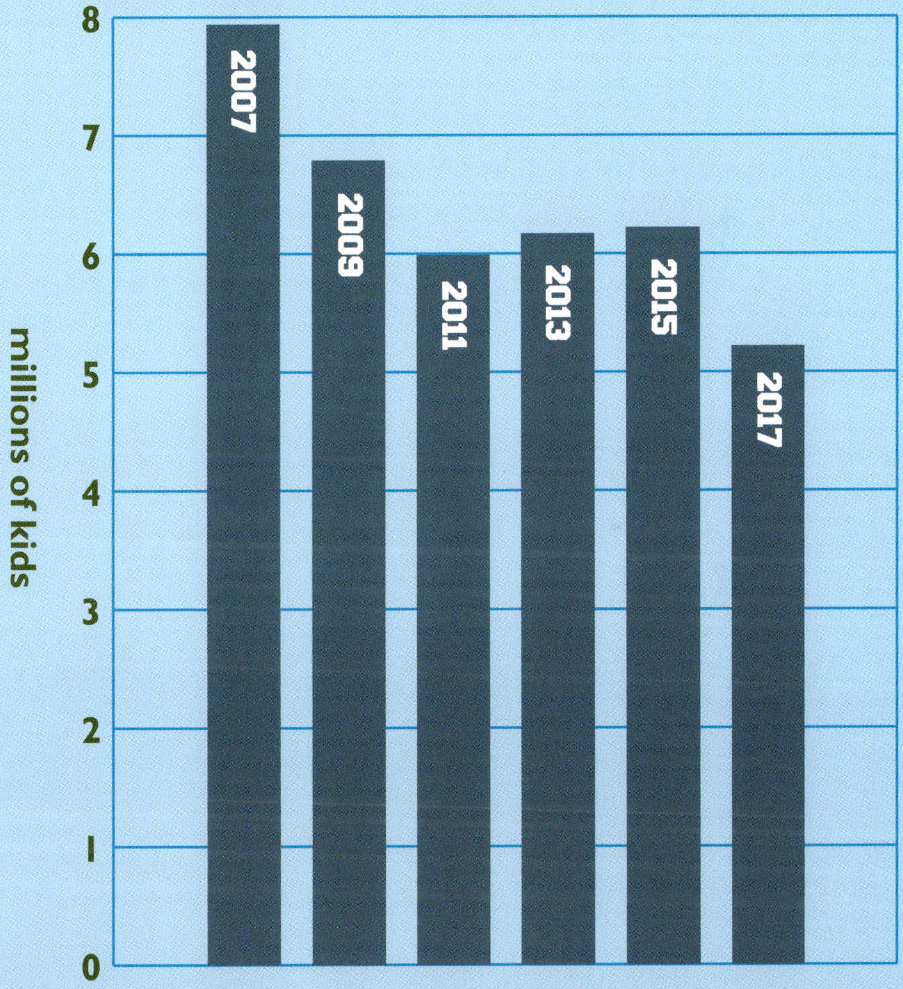

millions of kids

8
7
6
5
4
3
2
1
0

2007
2009
2011
2013
2015
2017

MAKING CONNECTIONS

TEXT-TO-SELF

Would you want to play tackle football? Why or why not?

TEXT-TO-TEXT

How does youth football compare to other youth sports you've read about?

TEXT-TO-WORLD

Football is one of the most popular sports for boys in the United States. But in many other countries, football is not popular. Why do you think that is?

GLOSSARY

ability – the skill to do something.

competitive – focused on winning a game or other activity.

develop – to grow or become more mature.

fundamentals – the basic skills of a game.

injury – a situation when someone gets hurt.

season – the time of year that people play a certain sport.

sprint – to run at full speed.

technique – a specific way of doing something, often requiring skill.

INDEX

Scan this code* and others like it while you read, or visit the website below to make this book pop!

popbooksonline.com/youth-football

*Scanning QR codes requires a web-enabled smart device with a QR code reader app and a camera.